Storyteller

100 Poem Letters

by Morgan Harper Nichols

Storyteller: 100 Poem Letters
By Morgan Harper Nichols

Cover Illustration and Design: Morgan Harper Nichols

For bookings and all other inquiries: www.morganharpernichols.com

From The Author:

Hello There,
I'm Morgan Harper Nichols, and I am so grateful you found this book. I am a writer, artist, and musician based in Los Angeles, California, where I reside with my husband Patrick Kekoa Nichols. I was born in L.A., but spent most of my childhood in Atlanta, Georgia where my parents James and Mona Harper served in full time ministry. My sister, Jamie-Grace Harper and I are both artists. Growing up, we were home schooled by our mother, who is also an artist. She taught us this: create something new everyday. I truly believe learning that at an early age is a huge part of what I create today and why I make it. I believe by making things, you can make a difference. By making things, you can tell a story, and inspire others to tell theirs, and I believe this is a gift from the Maker Himself. This is why I wrote and sang the song called "Storyteller" a few years ago. The meaning of that song inspired the poem letters in this book. Everyone has a story to tell. In what I make, what I write, and what I do, it is my prayer you are inspired to tell your story. *—Morgan Harper Nichols*

The mountain where I climbed,
The valley where I fell,
You were there all along,
That's the story I'll tell.
You brought the pieces together
and made me this storyteller,
now I know it is well, it is well,
that's the story I'll tell.
—Storyteller [The Song]
by Morgan Harper Nichols

About Storyteller: 100 Poem Letters:

For over a decade, many of the stories and poems I have written eventually turned into songs, and for that, I am grateful.

Over the past year, much of what I have written has turned into letters: letters to people, their stories, and the seasons they are in.

Even though I suppose, technically, what you will find in this book is considered poetry, I hope they read as letters: letters for people, places, things, seasons, years—letters for the story and for the storyteller.

There are one hundred poem letters in this book. I share them with you because I believe you have a story to tell, and I hope these poem letters encourage you to keep telling it. —*Morgan Harper Nichols*

For the storyteller:

Tell the story
of the mountain
you climbed.
Your words
could become a page
in someone else's
survival guide.
Morgan Harper Nichols

For the year:

When you start to feel
like things should have
been better this year,
remember the mountains and valleys
that got you here.
They are not accidents,
and those moments weren't in vain.
You are not the same.
You have grown, and you are growing,
you are breathing, you are living,
you are wrapped in
endless,
boundless,
grace.
And things will get better.
There is more to you
than yesterday.
Morgan Harper Nichols

For you:

For the highs and lows
and moments between,
mountains and valleys,
rivers and streams,
for where you are now
and where you will go,
for "I've always known,"
and "I told you so,"
for "nothing is happening,"
and "all has gone wrong,"
it is all in this journey
you will learn to be strong.
And to get where you are headed,
you are where you belong.
Morgan Harper Nichols

For the girl closing her eyes on the long train ride:

You may not be able
to bury your hardest times,
forgetting that they happened,
or change them down the line,
but because those times were hard,
they'll endure the moments when
you realize you are strong enough
to stand on top of them.
So wear your strongest posture now,
and see your hardest times
as more than just the times you fell
but a range of mountains
you learned to climb.
Morgan Harper Nichols

For the lone tree next to the side of the house:

I cannot tell you
what will happen
but I can tell you
it will be different
when the Light pours in.
Morgan Harper Nichols

For the one at home on Saturday:

It is okay if every weekend
does not lead to big moments
and campfires and laughter
that carries on for hours and hours.
Some weekends might be quiet, still,
with plenty of room to contemplate.
And in that contemplation room,
there is room to grow.
So hold those weekends dear.
Don't see them as less or as threats
to more exciting times.
There is beauty and truth
even in the seemingly mundane.
Morgan Harper Nichols

For "Courtney," sixteen years old:

Don't be troubled
by the mountain tops
you have yet to touch.
Like a tree, you will grow,
not from the sky,
but from the ground up.
Morgan Harper Nichols

For the forest:

In the wind
the tree will bend,
in the wind
the branch will shake,
but in the end,
the deeply rooted
will be
too strong
to break.
Morgan Harper Nichols

For the one letting go, moving on:

It's time to let it go,
float high above the hills
where you can finally breathe
and you finally heal.
Let this be your farewell,
a story you can tell
of just how far you've come
and how much more there is to go.
So let it go,
where you can finally breathe
and you finally heal.
Morgan Harper Nichols

For the one who has been
in the same place for years:

You will grow
even in this wasteland.
You will know
waiting in the valley.
You will hope
watering these seeds.
You still know
even in this wasteland,
You still grow.
Morgan Harper Nichols

For the one anticipating
what the rest of the year might bring:

And if everything
does not fall into place
at the same time and pace,
that does not mean
the years you've waited
have somehow been a waste.
Keep planting, sowing,
living, and knowing
beautiful things
take time...
and that's okay.
Morgan Harper Nichols

For the woman sitting in the coffee shop
while she fills out job applications:

I do not know why
some plants grow
in the sun, and some
in the shadows
but I do know
they still grow.
Morgan Harper Nichols

For the one looking through a travel book
right before the bookstore closes:

The bookstore is closing in ten minutes,
and on the opposite wall from where you stand
the cash register is closing.
Two workers are talking
about their weekend plans
and who has to come in tomorrow.
You flip through the final section of this book
you've been reading.
You're wanting to buy it,
but it's a bit expensive for your taste,
but the pictures and stories of this writer's travels
have you wondering...am I missing something?
But dearest friend,
don't be weary here.
You can take in these stories
and remember your favorite coffee
consumed only an hour ago
and feel that too is a valuable part of you.
The smooth pages filled with color
and the mere fact that you are here,
in peace and able to read,
is a world to explore
and get to know
all on its own,
all before the bookstore closes.
Morgan Harper Nichols

For the one who's been waiting for years:

Take deep breaths often.
You are going
to be okay.
The desert valley
has a river
for wellness
in the wait:
water living,
moving,
keeping the hearts that hunt
for better days.
Morgan Harper Nichols

For "Destiny," eighteen years old:

No matter the things
that have happened this year,
by grace there is still
a reason you're here.
Morgan Harper Nichols

For the open road:

Why do we love the open road,
yet simultaneously fear the unknown?
Perhaps it is because
the journey not yet taken
makes the heart a little worried,
but at the same exact time,
we know we need it.
We know there is only
so far we can go
unless we are willing
to faithfully face
what we do not yet know.
Morgan Harper Nichols

For the gardener:

You reap what you sow.
So sow well.
Sow seeds of faith
over seeds of doubt.
Sow seeds of peace
over seeds of worry.
Sow seeds of love
over seeds of fear.
And if in the past,
you sowed
what you did not need,
there is nothing that says
you must keep watering those things.
Leave them alone.
Let them die.
Make room to only sow things
that bring life.
Morgan Harper Nichols

For the one looking at old photographs:

When you look at the whole story
and where you've been,
be grateful
for slow and steady growth.
Be grateful
for those moments in the morning
to sit and think
and sink into thoughts
in that very moment:
rest,
reflect,
remember
just how far
you've come,
and how your story
is not over.
Morgan Harper Nichols

For the friend waiting for answers:

There is a time
for everything,
under the sun,
a time for everything.
So let Ecclesiastes sing
in the middle of the night,
in the wild
in the cold
in the back of your mind:
to you, my friend,
for all of time
there will be a time
for everything.
Morgan Harper Nichols

For the one who is far too often left out:

Adventure
is not tied
to who said
you could come along.
It is tied to the journey
you've been on
all along.
Morgan Harper Nichols

For the girl in the morning who feels unseen:

Open your bedroom blinds.
See the way the sun shines on you?
Blue or grey, Light fights through
and makes its way to you.
Now look around your room
and see the morning rising,
see the shadows falling
feel the day calling you:
to know you are loved,
to know you are seen,
to know faithful Light
is all you'll ever need.
Morgan Harper Nichols

For "Gina," twenty-two years old:

No matter the darkness
that runs the heart
to the ground,
grace continually
persists and abounds.
Morgan Harper Nichols

*For the woman sitting in traffic and
smiling, on her way to work:*

This year will not end
like last year at all.
You have learned to be free.
You have learned to be strong.
You have held onto light
when the night was too long.
You have braved many fears.
You learned a new song,
and through all of these valleys
you have learned to stand tall.
This year will not end
like last year at all.
Morgan Harper Nichols

For the one whose plans were changed
at the last minute:

Slow down.
There is no need to rush.
Take delight in these days
a minute at a time.
All of this a part of the process
of who you are becoming.
Morgan Harper Nichols

For the one arriving at home
after working overtime:

If things didn't turn out
like you hoped they would,
I hope, even here,
at sunset
you can fall in love
with the way light flickers
through the blinds
as it pushes through
the most persistent of shadows.
Graceful and intimidating movement
in every corner
of the room.
Even here,
I hope you will wake up
tomorrow morning
and unwrap each breath
like the gift it is,
and let no amount of worry
take one breath away.
Because in all of this,
there is still
more to you,
and going through things
you never thought
you'd go through
will only take you places
you never thought
you'd get to.
Morgan Harper Nichols

For the one who's past
rises in his mind far too often:

When you stumble on old vices
you are free to leave them there,
for not everything that rises
is worthy of your care.
So with every step you take,
run a shadow in the ground.
Dwell not on darker days
for things are different now.
Morgan Harper Nichols

For the woman who has overcome impossible things:

Over the trees, over the clouds,
over the things you could not figure out,
over the times you have been let down,
stop for a moment
and take a good look around.
You are moving north
in the mountains now.
Morgan Harper Nichols

For the girl who was left,
more than once
by the same person,
without any explanation:

In her lowest place
she found the grace,
the strength, the courage,
the room, the space
to move and live
and breathe again.
Morgan Harper Nichols

For the one learning to be brave:

Take deep breaths
and take your time
for this mountain here
you will learn to climb.

You will learn to brave
these all new heights,
you will grow in grace,
you will be alright.

You will learn to see
the world from here:
a thousand miles
above your fears.
Morgan Harper Nichols

For the one who has found school
to be far more difficult than she expected this year:

She will not be afraid
when things do not make sense.
For day by day
she will make it through this.
She will walk tall, with strength,
and new found wisdom.
She will not be afraid
when things do not make sense.
Morgan Harper Nichols

For time spent at home:

If you were to count
the things
you learned
in this space
this year,
you would be here
for hours.
Sometimes
it might just be better
to sit,
and look
and wonder
and breathe,
being grateful
for all of the little things
and the beautiful truth
that you made it this far.
Morgan Harper Nichols

For the one with high hopes for seasons to come:

Hear the wind as it howls around you
over the ridges and into the valley
where you stand in the drying weeds,
with a sense of new days coming.
See the setting sun
turning barren lands
into rows of endless yellow
that now has you thinking,
maybe the change of a season
is more than sorrow,
but a leap, a promise
for hope
tomorrow.
Morgan Harper Nichols

For the one who is tired,
about to head home
from a long day of work:

Cars and their engines
ramble on a few streets over,
but beyond fading echoes,
you hear nothing at all,
as the smell of baker's bread
sweeps down the street where you stand,

overhead are rows and rows of draping lights
that seem to call for celebration.

But you see only setting skies
and your scar that has not healed
and the feeling that you've gone too far
is all that you can feel.

But as the sky closes in
and the day escapes,
I hope that you can see
the lights that hang above you
have only gotten a little brighter,
and there is still plenty of time
for you to make it home.
Morgan Harper Nichols

For the writer:

Writing is a chance
to speak to those
who don't feel spoken to,
and put into words
what the readers thought
they were alone
in thinking about.
Morgan Harper Nichols

For the one in a new city:

Sometimes
the best way
to get to know a city
is to step out of its way.
Stare tall at its cathedrals
tucked in corners on narrow streets
and say nothing.
Feel the history
in the languages
coming from the bustling shops
and taste the food
as it floats through
the morning air.
Walk, talk, smell, see
until you forget sometimes
to take a photograph
or to write it down
because you were just
too busy
living.
Morgan Harper Nichols

For the one admiring
vintage maps:

You can make notes
of the well known streets
and draw out trails
from well traveled paths,
but even then,
even the most detailed maps in the world
can only reveal so much to you.

Until you get up and go,
stepping out boldly into the unknown,
you have absolutely no idea
of what all you will find.

But that's the beauty of traveling through life.
This is how you will learn to stay strong.

We don't have to know everything
to know that taking
brave and faithful steps
will lead us where we belong.
Morgan Harper Nichols

For "Amy," living in a country far from home:

After all this time
she is learning to see,
she is so much stronger
than she thought she would be.
Morgan Harper Nichols

For the nineteen year old who doesn't know what to do
after her plans have fallen through, in autumn:

More than you see
the way things haven't worked out,
more than you see
the unwritten page of the chapter
you are anxious to complete,
see all around you the change that is happening.
See the way the leaves color and burn
and the many things in this season
you are going to learn,
because just as there are
a hundred unread the books on the shelf
there are one hundred things
you do not yet know about yourself.

And that is okay.
In fact, it is supposed to be that way.
This is change.
And it is a beautiful thing.
You are still growing,
into who you are meant to be.
Morgan Harper Nichols

For the man with a face flushed red,
and his hand on his forehead thinking deeply,
as he sits in traffic:

The rush of the day
has slowed down
to nothing more
than lanes of cars
inching forward
all too slowly
on the interstate.

In this moment,
you ask no questions.
You only think
of all invested
and what it takes
to make it home
to take a break
just for the night.

But even though uncertain things
have flooded your mind,
peace is not the fleeting kind.
It never leaves on days like this.
It sticks around on days like this
reminding you
there is more than this.
Morgan Harper Nichols

For the forty-five-year-old woman
in the music store
buying her first guitar:

And just like that,
you will carry on.
Even when you were
overlooked
and profoundly
underestimated.
By grace, with strength,
you will carry on.
You will sing new songs.
You will give all you have,
and for the rest of time,
you will be alright.
Because if nothing else,
darkness taught you:
grace was the fire
burning wild
and unbridled
in your tired heart.
And now you are here.
You are over the bridge.
Free.
Morgan Harper Nichols

For the woman telling a story to her friend
on a morning walk:

You may remember
everything about this morning,
or you may remember
none of it at all,
but if nothing else,
it is good for you to have this space
to walk it out and talk it through.
Because far too often
the world has felt too big,
and there was a time
when you felt helpless,
crowded and alone all at once.
But now you are here,
and you know at least one person,
on at least one day,
who found at least one moment
to walk, to talk, and listen.
Because sometimes
it's just these candid conversations
in faithful morning light
that remind us we are not alone
and we are going to be alright.
Morgan Harper Nichols

For the one who has made it
through impossible things:

Breathe deep
in newfound hope,
and be forever changed.
For Light has found
Its way to you,
and you will never
be the same.
Morgan Harper Nichols

For the one who loves unconditionally:

More than she
was known
for her accomplishments,
she was known
for the way
she loved.
Morgan Harper Nichols

For the girl gardening with her grandmother
in the front yard:

In front of the yellow house
you wore green gloves
as you tended to the weeds
growing near the sidewalk.
You talked with your grandmother
about some of the things
that happened that week,
and what you were feeling,
and what Grandpa might've thought,
because it's days like this, you miss him.
And as you brush the soil
from the hem of your sleeve,
light shines through the flowers
and their tiniest of leaves.
You look down to the ground,
and you start to see
growth takes time
but it is all grace-breathed,
slow and steady.
It is still happening,
right here, new life,
right before your eyes.
Morgan Harper Nichols

For the girl on my flight
leaning into her window seat,
enthralled by the rows of city lights
rolling out beneath her feet:

If you happen to feel small
in this sea of rolling lights,
this feeling is more than fear,
this feeling is *alive,*
permission to be free,
well traveled and well rested,
to think a billion thoughts
while at the same time speechless.
Morgan Harper Nichols

For the woman turning twenty-four
a few tables over from me
at the restaurant:

I hope this is day one
of a beautiful year
of chasing light,
and abandoning fears,
a brand new chapter
that started right here.
I hope you can look back on this day,
and remember even though life
was not perfect back then
you were smiling,
laughing,
present
with friends,
and these are the moments
you will hold to the end.
No matter what changes
no matter what happens,
this will always be the place
a new chapter began.
Morgan Harper Nichols

For the night before her birthday:

Take heart.
The value of your life
is not measured
in calendar years.
Morgan Harper Nichols

For the wildflower:

The sun is still shining,
the wind is still blowing,
and out in the wild
you are growing.
Days may go by
without change
you can feel,
but what's happening here
is most certainly real:
You are becoming
what you were meant
to become
out in the wild
in the arms of the sun.
Morgan Harper Nichols

For the girl in Babylon:

May you raise
your hands
in Babylon.
Find grace
out in the wild.
Make a song
from nothing.
Have hope.
There's more
to come.
Morgan Harper Nichols

For this moment:

Even if the wait
carries on another year,
I will not get where I am going
without first learning
to be here.
Morgan Harper Nichols

For the older woman, in awe at the Grand Canyon:

Through all these
caves and canyons
and things
you do not understand,
may you find
the peace and freedom
on tethered grounds,
the strength to stand.
Morgan Harper Nichols

For the girl who noticed the butterfly:

And now she knows that confidence
does not lie in what appears,
but in the strength and courage
growing in her heart for years.
Morgan Harper Nichols

For the one wondering what a new month holds:

She will not worry,
she will be just fine.
She will brave the new season
one day at a time.
Morgan Harper Nichols

For the girl driving home late at night:

When there are street lamps and headlights
guiding you home
and you're tired and weary of being alone,
breathe deep and hold on
and do not let go just yet.
For even though it's late and you do not know
how much longer you can wait,
how much more you can take,
keep your eyes on the road.
Keep your eyes on the light.
Carry on another day,
carry on another night.
You will make it through this.
You will be alright.
By grace, with light,
you will be alright.
Morgan Harper Nichols

For who I was, three days ago:

I thought I was caving in,
but I was actually
being broken in
so I could begin again.
Morgan Harper Nichols

For the one fighting the good fight:

I have this crazy hope
that these walls can be painted
in colors so bright
that all they see in you
is Light.
Burdened by shadows no more,
I hope you can walk
through those doors,
anchored to hope,
and Eternal Love:
protected,
guided,
held
forever.
And even when their words
pierce beneath
your toughest skin,
I hope you know
they cannot dim
the hope
the Light
burning
within.
Morgan Harper Nichols

For the those who do not feel
they have much work with right now:

I hope tomorrow
is the day
you can wake up and say,
"I do not have a lot,
but I do know
time and time again,
the sun has continued
to shine on me."
Morgan Harper Nichols

For the abandoned storefront painted in blue:

For awhile it seemed
too good to be true.
When they painted the walls,
and put up the sign,
it felt like things
were for real this time.
But something happened
between then and now,
and there are still those days
you try to figure out:
"Where did everyone go?
Why did everyone leave?
Who are all these people
carrying on
without me?
I watch as they pass,
and they say so many things,
but they stop and say
nothing to me."

Oh, dear abandoned storefront in blue,
they may not know you,
but you are still you.
Your walls have been woven
in the tapestry of this city,
and no matter the things
that have changed
this year,
by grace,
there is still
a reason
you're here.
Morgan Harper Nichols

For the teenage friends shopping together for books:

If someday
someone grows up
or moves away,
and you don't all get to
read the same books
laugh the same laughs
take the same trips:
never let go of these moments.
Because these moments
are still written
in the binds of time.
You can still grow here,
learn here,
be here,
with your friends
and hold these moments
until the end.
Because many years from now,
these days will still matter.
They will each have a chapter
in the stories you gather.
Morgan Harper Nichols

For the colors running pink and blue
on unexpected blank envelopes:

You rise in the morning
exploding from a can made of tin,
your colors running thin
beyond the borders
of an unexpected canvas.
Unsure of where you'd land,
I wore gloves to keep the colors,
like water, at bay.
But your colors are the kind to run free,
and they got to my hands
anyway.
Morgan Harper Nichols

For the child swinging on the railing
at the restaurant, while waiting for his parents:

Years from now,
you might not remember this exact moment:
the way the daylight fell on you
while you were waiting,
and the way the wind was blowing
even when you were still.
But this small, simple moment in time is a part of you.
You will go on to have many other moments.
You will go on to live in different years.
You will go on to face and conquer many fears,
and most of all, you will grow
in thousands of moments wrapped in the life of one,
living, breathing, carrying on.
Morgan Harper Nichols

For the bright, colorful mural by the beach:

Unexpected colors step into view:
yellows and oranges
against a sky, soft and blue.
I suppose you did not ask
to be painted this way,
but you wear this story
and these colors so well.
You wear them as though
you have something to tell.
Because even when we do not choose
how we have been painted in some way,
we walk away with this:
"I do not know why
things turned out this way,
but I do know I now
have something to say."
Morgan Harper Nichols

For the one moving far away from everything she knows:

I hope the simplest of times
you have with those you love,
the random moment you burst into laughter,
and the day you chose to keep smiling
for no reason at all,
are just little things
along the way
to remind you
all of these moments
matter too.
And I hope you take that with you,
diving deep into the wonder of day,
journeying out to sea
in boundless ocean blue,
wrapped in endless grace,
unafraid of uncertainty,
approaching bravely
the day.
I hope you remember
every day
this way.
Morgan Harper Nichols

For the seventeen-year-old girl:

Confidence flourishes
in abandoning the idea
we need to look like
we have it all together.
Morgan Harper Nichols

For the kid starting at a brand-new school:

If you ever start to doubt
you belong here,
I want you to know
this place is yours too.
There may be people
who brush by
and see straight through you,
but don't let that stop you.
You belong here too.
Morgan Harper Nichols

For the family driving toward the mountains,
in the northern part of the state:

While the face of the mountain
is seen for many miles,
the foot of the mountain
is pitted deep in the wild,
for climbing always
begins on the ground.
Morgan Harper Nichols

For "Rachel," the girl who has never known romantic love:

The same exact Light that shines on the one
who is falling in love, who is getting engaged,
who is walking down the aisle on her wedding day,
the same exact Light shines on you all the same.

And nothing and no one can take that away.

No matter the one was too busy, too focused,
too far away to notice,
or slowly deciding he was not ready,
or he wanted something
you could not give,
or you were left hanging
with words left unsaid,
or if the timing was wrong
and he moved on instead,

the same exact Light shines on you all the same.

And one day there will be
someone brave enough to see
he can follow the Way, the Light
right to your heart.

Because no matter what happened
before that day,

the same exact Light that is shining on you,
will be shining on him all the same.
Morgan Harper Nichols

For friends of mine:

Remember that time
you smiled
for no reason
and laughed about something
that happened forever ago?
Keep doing that.
Morgan Harper Nichols

For "Andrea," twenty-eight years old:

Just because
they're succeeding
before you,
doesn't mean
they're succeeding
in replacement of you.
There will still be
a place for you.
There will always be
a place for you.
Morgan Harper Nichols

For the girl staring up at grey skies,
as the taxi drives her to the airport:

All she wanted was
to get this part of the journey over with,
to feel a little accomplished,
after all the work she's put in.
She is quiet, but she is thinking loud,
counting task by task
like trees in a forest sprouting high
within her head.
Oh how she longs for this ride to end,
so she can finally go somewhere else instead.
But until she gets there,
she will learn to count these moments
not as a loss,
but as the time she needed
to make it across
the mountain range of things
stretched out before her.
And she knows soon enough,
she will make it there,
but for now,
she will wait.
She will rest.
Morgan Harper Nichols

For the server cleaning off her last table
right before the restaurant
closes for the evening:

The year is leaving you again,
and the stack of things
you did not do
are piling up again.

But remember tonight
in the silhouette of power lines,
that even though the sun
is slipping from the sky
there is still time,
plenty of time
to run, to hope,
in the middle of the night,
to wake in the morning
to all-new light.
My dear, oh my dear,
there is still time,
plenty of time
to live.
Morgan Harper Nichols

For the twelve-year-old me:

Traveling the world is not limited to
open roads and airport codes.
There's a world inside the bounds of books
far too often overlooked.
Your library card is a passport too.
Morgan Harper Nichols

For the one in the thrift store
on a Wednesday morning:

You never tire
of old books,
looking for them
in yard sales
and thrift stores,
even the ones
you've read before.
Because there's something
to the way
the older pages feel,
and the way they peel
where the bind is worn and broken in:
this is where the story begins.
A bit like childhood
all over again.
And you will find the time
to read this book,
forget all the troubles,
and somehow be changed
all over again.
Morgan Harper Nichols

For the girl in line at the bank:

The light
you see
in her
comes from
this place
within her
where she
believes
by faith
that after
everything,
she is still
somehow
going
to
be
okay.
Morgan Harper Nichols

For the rest of this month:

Do not just wait
to be invited to something.
Create something.
Contribute something.
Make something.
Do something.
Morgan Harper Nichols

For the one with the broken heart:

Maybe if you had been different,
you would have been what they wanted.
But maybe if you have been what they wanted,
you would have been different
than who you were supposed to be.
Morgan Harper Nichols

For the weary soul:

Maybe you were made
for this very moment,
to walk bravely
through blazing fire,
and by grace,
come forth
as gold.
Morgan Harper Nichols

For "Maria:"

Things will look different now
for your soul's been changed for good,
and you will not fall apart
even though you thought you would.
For even though
you do not feel
as strong as you used to be
you are finding hope,
for this new season
is exactly what you need.
Morgan Harper Nichols

For the woman with the canceled flight:

There was this moment in time
where she begin to understand
the path might look different
than she was expecting.
But it did not stop
her continual treading.
It did not mean
she was lost.

So she stopped
and settled
on this:

I will travel.
I will move.
I will proceed,
wrapped in endless grace,
headed where I am meant to be.
Morgan Harper Nichols

For the older gentlemen
checking shoppers' receipts at the door
of the discount department store:

If we were counting our decades
one by one
with our fingers:
one, two, three, four, five, six, seven...
both of your hands
would be close to fully open
to wave hello,
to take receipts,
to wave goodbye,
to hold a piece
of all the stories
your smile and laugh
has touched, because
through all the things
you have made it through,
through all these years
you have lived.
Morgan Harper Nichols

For the forgotten:

They can take a lot of things,
but they cannot take your hope.
They cannot take the freedom
stirring deep within your soul.
Morgan Harper Nichols

For the seafarer in the morning, a prayer:

Untied from my ship's allotted place
I float far into boundless ocean blue
between land and air
in waves and wonders.
I come in search of You,
for You have made me aware
that my soul You have kept
eternally anchored
to Your glorious depth.
Morgan Harper Nichols

For the one who was not believed in:

Years from now,
there will be people
who finally realize
they should given you a chance.
They will finally see
that you were worth more
than they willing to accept,
and there was more to you
than they were willing to see.
But don't do what you do
for those people.
Don't do what you do
to prove them wrong.
Do what you do for The One
who has always been there all along.
Morgan Harper Nichols

For the one who has never come in first place:

Your importance,
your worth,
your usefulness
is not positioned
based on where others are
or what they are doing.
You are not above anyone else.
You are not beneath them either.
Your value can never, ever be ranked.
Morgan Harper Nichols

For the one in the valley:

You may have been
waiting in this valley
for the same things
for years,
but keep your eyes open.
Something new
is happening here.
Morgan Harper Nichols

For the one scrolling through photos of the beach:

Fix your eyes
on Love Eternal,
and be reminded
of the endlessness.
Fix your eyes
on boundless sea,
quickly forgetting
the worries of morning.
Make the most of ordinary days,
and find some way
to leap with abandon
into never ending hope.
Find beauty and life
in the seemingly mundane,
with or without
an ocean's wave.
Morgan Harper Nichols

For the teenager shopping with her dad
as he is dancing in the store:

Remember the silly,
the candid,
the random.
It's okay to break loose
once in awhile,
with the day
unplanned.
You need these kind
of moments too,
and these moments also
need you.
Morgan Harper Nichols

For the girl by the vending machine
at the truckstop in the desert,
near the interstate exit:

You thought you'd see stars
in the desert tonight,
but the cars rolling past
bear too many lights.
As shadows build high
behind exit signs,
the road is narrowing
and your eyes are growing wide.

You pull off the exit
unsure if you're lost,
for you're only a child
in search of the cost:
how many quarters
for the vending machine
to buy you more time
to find what you need?

But deep in the night
I hope you will find
the strength and courage
to sleep and unwind.
And in the morning
you will wake up to see
the road, still there, to take you
exactly where you need to be.
Morgan Harper Nichols

For the little boy in a war-torn land,
sleeping in the stairwell:

I do not know how you sleep so well
at the bottom of the stairwell,
out in the open
in the foothills of explosions.
I see strength in you
no one has ever seen in me.
Who am I to think
I have anything figured out at all,
when you can sleep so peacefully
on a stairwell in a street.
Morgan Harper Nichols

For the neighbor:

On the days we are fine,
at least one of our neighbors is not.
It can be easy to dismiss
the necessity of a kind word
when we are not the one in need.
But the reality is this:
there are people roaming the city
who have not been loved in years.
There are people roaming the city
who have not been loved in years.
Morgan Harper Nichols

For the sixteen year old
checking out a book from the library
about writing fantasy fiction:

The world may be a crowded place,
but there is still room for you,
room for you to tell your story
and to create things and contribute things
that make a difference.
Your age does not matter.
Where you were raised
does not matter.
You are on this earth for a reason.
You are not just taking up space.
There will be no perfect moment
before you take the leap
and speak.
Morgan Harper Nichols

For the girl telling her friends goodbye
as she walks home, alone:

When night has settled into itself
and all of the friends have said goodbye,
and you're left to wrestle
those same old thoughts
with a playlist looping
those same old songs.
If all of these nights
seem to all end the same
may you learn to be able
to see it this way:
beauty can still be found
in the seemingly mundane,
and you are still growing,
even in subtle change.
Morgan Harper Nichols

For the girl, exhausted, standing in the checkout line,
reading a long text message on her phone:

The chaos of the day
caused her to withdraw,
and shut out the world.
She was certain now
she was empty, drained,
and in her heart, she fell.

But she did not fail,
for when she fell,
she fell into grace.
Morgan Harper Nichols

For the one in the place of hope deferred:

She will stand tall
on the rooftops of her worries
and proclaim into the depth
of a starless night:
"I will make it through this.
By grace, I will be alright."
Morgan Harper Nichols

For the one who is praying:

One day you will wake up
and all of the waiting
will have made sense.
You will realize
all of the prayers
that seemed to be
tangled in worries
were actually wrapped tightly
in God's grace.
You will realize that
even though before
you were certain it was over,
you were actually...okay,
and everything
that was supposed to happen,
happened,
and you are right where
you need to be.
Morgan Harper Nichols

For the dreamer:

Not everyone believes in her.
not everyone supports her,
but her God goes with her,
and that's what sustains her.
Morgan Harper Nichols

For the one searching for more:

If life were but a sum
of fast moving trains
and aerial views of cityscapes,
then tell me, what would there be to gain?
What would there be to look forward to
if everything were laid out before you,
and opening a hand was all you had to do?
Slowly, but inevitably, you would
overlook the most beautiful things.
You would no longer see the story of things
that took time before they came to be.
You would make light of moments
that made you yourself,
failing to see that you are not
a polished artifact on a shelf,
but clay in the hands of the Potter Himself,
on a wheel, spinning through and through.
Though it feels, at times, it is out of control,
it is actually the tangible process
of Him making you whole,
into something much more
than a series of moments
too good to be true.
It is slow intentional process
of Him showing you the real you.
Morgan Harper Nichols

For The One:

You are the reason
I am still breathing,
though I am feeling torn apart.
You are the Hallelujah beating
through my broken, weary heart.
Morgan Harper Nichols

For the young sailor, finding her way home:

In onward, beautiful,
lateral movement,
her worries collapsed in lines
of crackled white foam on the coast.

She takes a deep breath
as she finally realizes
how far she's come
from the nights she spent
out on the ocean alone.
In the morning,
boundless water and worry
are stirred no more.
And now she is certain,
she will make it home.
She will learn to let go.
She will hold her ear to the Voice of The One
Who has told her so:

"Let your worries be like waves
swelling up in the wind
breaking off on the shore.
Their crested shapes
now lines of foam in the sand
and nothing more."
Morgan Harper Nichols

For the wanderer:

You will go through seasons
of sun and wind and rain.
You will tread the desert,
and in and out of pain.
You will go through years
wondering if you're good enough.
But you will never go too far
that you are outside of My Love.
Morgan Harper Nichols

...and, lo, I am with you always, even unto the end of the world
– Matthew 28:20 KJV

Thank you for reading. Let's stay in touch.

Sincerely,
Morgan Harper Nichols

morganharpernichols.com
facebook.com/morganharpernichols
instagram.com/morganharpernichols
youtube.com/morganharpernichols
pinterest.com/morganharperichols
anchor.fm/morganharpernichols
twitter.com/morganhnichols
snapchat.com/add/morganhnichols

Podcast:
The Morgan Harper Nichols Show
on iTunes and Google Play

Music:
morganharpernichols.com/music

For bookings and all other inquiries,
find more information at:
morganharpernichols.com

Made in the USA
Lexington, KY
03 November 2019